Where does it come from?

Sweater

Illustrated by
Diane Tippell

Macdonald

There's wool growing on these hills.
That's right. It's on the sheep.
Their fleeces are made of lots of very
fine hair which is used to make wool
for us to wear.

It is important that insects which can make the sheep ill don't make their homes in the sheep's fleeces. So the shepherds wash the sheep in a special bath called a sheep dip.

When their fleeces are long, the sheep are clipped. The sheep shearers hold each sheep tightly between their legs while they run their electric clippers over it to cut the fleece off. It's just like having a short hair cut. It doesn't hurt.

The woman at the table is checking each fleece and pulling off the loose bits. Some of the wool is quite muddy from the fields. It's greasy too. The grease was keeping the sheep dry when it rained. Now the fleeces are rolled up and put into big bags to be taken to the wool factory.

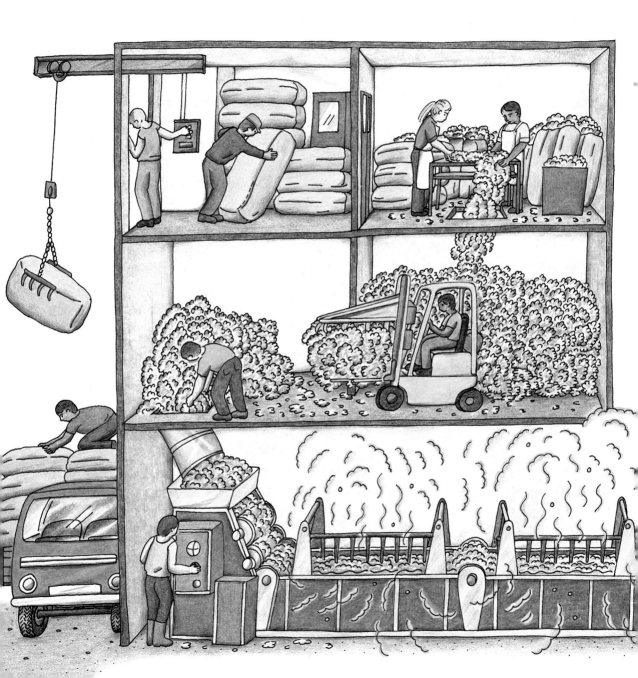

This is the wool factory. The bags of fleeces are lifted in from the lorry by a crane. On the top floor the sorters open the bags and sort out the fleeces. They drop them through holes in the floor into the rooms below. There the forklift truck drivers scoop up the wool and drop it down to the bottom floor to be washed.

It's very hot and smelly down here. There's steam everywhere from the huge machine that washes the grease and dirt out of the wool. Its spikes move backwards and forwards, pushing the wool through tanks of hot soapy water, with rollers squeezing the dirt out in between. At the end the wool goes into a giant hot-air dryer and becomes soft and white. This dryer seems to need unblocking!

Now they're clean and dry the fluffy lumps of wool need to be untangled. It's rather like brushing a bad tangle out of your hair. The first machine has spiky rollers which tease the wool out so that any bits of grass or twigs that are still caught up in it can be brushed off.

Next the drawing machines stretch the wool out.
The combing machine combs through the tiny hairs
that make up the wool until they are straight at last.
And finally the machines at the end wind the thick ribbon of
wool into big tube-shaped balls.

This is the part of the factory where the balls of wool are dyed different colours. Each ball is packed tightly into a metal cylinder with holes in it. When the man presses his control button, the crane lifts the cylinder into a huge vat. It's like a saucepan with a very tight lid.

The coloured dye is mixed up and pumped into the vat. It has to be hot and pumped very hard to make sure the colour gets right through the wool. When the time is up the vat switches itself off. The wool is lifted out. It's hot and wet and brightly coloured.

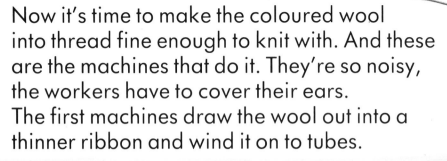

Now it's time to make the coloured wool into thread fine enough to knit with. And these are the machines that do it. They're so noisy, the workers have to cover their ears.
The first machines draw the wool out into a thinner ribbon and wind it on to tubes.

Then the workers put the tubes on the spinning machines. First the wool is spun out until it's very fine, then twisted together, two threads at a time, to make it stronger. The workers have to keep loose fluff out of the machines and make sure the thread hasn't broken.

The wool is nearly ready to use. This last machine winds it from the big tubes into small balls. It puts labels round each ball and counts them out ready for the packers to put in plastic bags for the shops.

The bags of wool are stored in the warehouse and the shops order what they need from here. The women take the right bags of wool for each order off the shelves and pack them in big brown paper bags ready to be delivered to the shops by lorry.

Here's the wool arriving at the shop. Tom and his grandmother have come to choose some wool for a new sweater. It's hard when there are so many different kinds and colours to choose from. Tom sees the new wool from the factory being unpacked. "Let's have that!" he says.

Now they only have to choose the pattern for the sweater and some knitting needles and they'll be ready to go. Tom's brother Michael asks if he can have one just the same.

Grandmother is busy knitting Tom's sweater. She's made the front and the sleeves. Now she's knitting the back. Tom is trying to put the pieces together.

"They don't look much like a sweater to me," he says.

"Well they've still got to be sewn up," says his gran.

"Now do you believe me?" Tom's sweater is finished at last and he is very pleased. It's just what he needs with winter coming. Michael can't wait for his to be ready too.